go! CHINESE 听说读打写

Heleinke / Su hin

Go 300

Workbook
(Simplified Character Edition)

罗秋昭
Julie LO

薛意梅
Emily YIH

CENGAGE
Learning™

Andover • Melbourne • Mexico City • Stamford, CT • Toronto • Hong Kong • New Delhi • Seoul • Singapore • Tokyo

Go! Chinese Go300 Workbook
(Simplified Character Edition)
Julie Lo, Emily Yih

Publishing Director, CLT Product Director:
Paul K. H. Tan

Editorial Manager:
Lan Zhao

Associate Development Editor:
Coco Koh

Editor:
Titus Teo

Senior Graphic Designer:
Melvin Chong

Senior Product Manager (Asia):
Joyce Tan

Product Manager (Outside Asia):
Mei Yun Loh

Assistant Publishing Manager:
Pauline Lim

Production Executive:
Cindy Chai

Account Manager (China):
Arthur Sun

Assistant Editor, ELT:
Yuan Ting Soh

ISBN-13: 978-981-4246-47-7
ISBN-10: 981-4246-47-6

Cengage Learning Asia Pte Ltd
5 Shenton Way #01-01
UIC Building
Singapore 068808

Cengage Learning is a leading provider of customized learning solutions with office locations around the globe, including Andover, Melbourne, Mexico City, Stamford (CT), Toronto, Hong Kong, New Delhi, Seoul, Singapore, and Tokyo Locate your local office at **www.cengage.com/global**

Cengage Learning products are represented in Canada by Nelson Education, Ltd.

For product information, visit **www.cengagesasia.com**

Photo credits
Cover: © Charly Franklin/Taxi/Getty Images.

Printed in Singapore
2 3 4 5 14 13 12 11

Preface

Go! Chinese, together with *IQChinese Go* multimedia CD-ROM, is a fully integrated Chinese language program that offers an easy, enjoyable, and effective learning experience for learners of Chinese as a foreign language.

The Workbook is an essential component of the *Go! Chinese* series. The exercises are closely linked to the content of each lesson, allowing students to solidify their understanding of and review the lesson learned in the classroom.

The Workbook features the following types of exercises:

- **Foundation Building Exercises**

  Phonetics (*pinyin*), Chinese radicals, vocabulary review, sentence re-ordering, and translation are examples of foundation building exercises. These exercises help students systematically build a solid foundation in the Chinese language.

- **Problem-Solving Exercises**

  Exercises such as crossword puzzles, composing short conversations, and answering questions involving the interpretation of graphs or pictures, provide students with interesting and challenging opportunities to learn the Chinese language through problem-solving tasks.

- **Chinese Typing Exercises**

  The unique characteristic of this series is the use of Chinese typing as an instructional strategy to improve word recognition, listening, and pronunciation skills. The typing activity can be found in the CD-ROM. Students are asked to type characters or sentences as they are read aloud or displayed on the computer screen. They will be alerted if they make a mistake and will be given the chance to correct them. If they do not get it right on the third try, the software provides immediate feedback on how to correct the error. This interactive trial-and-error process allows students to develop self-confidence and learn by doing. Students can use the chart in the Workbook to record their best timings for these typing activities (Sentence Quiz). Students can also separately keep a list of words that they frequently have trouble with for future review.

  The Sentence Quiz exercise comprises four levels.

  ➤ Level 1 – Warm-up Quiz (Look, Listen, and Type): Chinese text, *pinyin*, and audio prompts are provided.

  ➤ Level 2 – Visual-aid Quiz: Only Chinese text is provided. There are no *pinyin* or audio prompts.

  ➤ Level 3 – Audio-aid Quiz: Only audio prompts are provided.

  ➤ Level 4 – Character-selection Quiz: Only Chinese text is provided. After entering the correct *pinyin*, students are required to select the correct character from a list of similar looking characters.

Besides the Sentence Quiz exercises, students can practice Chinese typing in the "Teacher's Assignment" section of the CD-ROM. In these exercises, teachers can vary the level of difficulty based on the students' proficiency level. However, students can only type in numerals and Chinese characters they have learned before. For example, in level Go300, students can only type in Chinese characters* that they have learned in levels Go100 to Go300. Upon completion, the exercises are printable, and there is a time-recording feature to indicate the completion time of each activity. A number of exercises in the Workbook may be completed in the "Teacher's Assignment" section.

* Core vocabulary only; does not include supplementary vocabulary taught in the Textbook.

• Word Recognition and Character Writing Exercises

To help students learn to read and recognize actual Chinese characters, *pinyin* is generally not annotated in the Workbook, except for certain *pinyin*, writing, and vocabulary exercises.

The Workbook also provides Chinese character writing worksheets for a subset of the vocabulary to help students understand and appreciate the characteristics and formation of Chinese characters. Writing can help students remember the Chinese characters better. The writing sheets illustrate the correct stroke order of each character. Grid lines and traceable characters are also provided to help students trace and copy characters until they are able to write them independently. The teacher may assign additional character writing practice according to her classroom emphasis and needs.

• Review Units

Two Review units are provided after every five lessons in the Workbook. They give students the opportunity to review and reflect on their knowledge and progress, and reinforce what they have learned. Teachers may have students work on these units individually as homework, or go over them together in class.

The Workbook is designed to enable students to complete all exercises independently, either in class, or at home. Students should not have to spend more than 15 minutes on each page. Teachers may also wish to encourage students to spend 10 minutes a day on the Sentence Quiz exercises in the CD-ROM.

Table of Contents

PREFACE iii

LESSON 1　我的家人
My Family 1

LESSON 2　学校活动
School Activities 7

LESSON 3　用心做好
Try Your Best 13

LESSON 4　我生病了
I Am Sick 19

LESSON 5　家在哪里?
Where Is Your Home? 25

REVIEW 1 31

LESSON 6　我的心情
My Moods 37

LESSON 7　我看球赛
Watching a Ball Game 43

LESSON 8　我的爱好
My Hobbies 49

LESSON 9　电视节目
Television Programs 55

LESSON 10　今天天气
The Weather Today 62

REVIEW 2 68

LESSON 1

我的家人
My Family

1 For each word, write down the *pinyin* in the second column. In the third column, write down "男" if the term refers to a male and "女" if it refers to a female.

Chinese	*Pinyin*	Gender
① 舅舅	jiù jiu	男
② 伯伯	bó bo	男
③ 叔叔	shū shu	男
④ 奶奶	nǎi nai	女
⑤ 爷爷	yé ye	男
⑥ 姨妈	yí mā	女
⑦ 外婆	Wài Pó	女
⑧ 外公	Wài gōng	男

2 Which of the following terms address your paternal relatives (Father's family) and which terms address your maternal relatives (Mother's family)? Categorize them in the spaces provided below.

爷爷　　外婆　　姑姑　　舅舅　　叔叔
姨妈　　伯伯　　堂哥　　奶奶　　外公

Father's Family

爷爷
奶奶
伯伯
姑姑
叔叔

Mother's Family

外公
外婆
舅舅
姨妈

3 Go to *Exercise > Sentence Quiz* in your ⟨Go 300⟩ to take the quiz. Choose the best two results.

TYPING RECORDS		Date	Accurate Spelling per Minute	Three Most Common Mistakes (Character)
	Record 1			
		Level	Time Elapsed	
	Record 2	Date	Accurate Spelling per Minute	Three Most Common Mistakes (Character)
		Level	Time Elapsed	

4 Fill in the blanks with the words below.

> Ⓐ 就是　　Ⓑ 都是　　Ⓒ 也是

① 爸爸的妈妈 _就是_ 我的奶奶。

② 姐姐、弟弟和我 _都是_ 一家人。

③ 爸爸是伯伯的弟弟，叔叔 _也是_ 伯伯的弟弟。

④ 我是爷爷的孙女，妹妹 _也是_ 爷爷的孙女。

⑤ 我是外公的外孙， _也是_ 外婆的外孙。

⑥ 外公的儿子 _就是_ 我的舅舅。

⑦ 姨妈和妈妈 _都是_ 外公的女儿。

5 Pick the odd one out.

① (姨) ❶ 叔叔　　❷ 奶奶　　❸ 堂哥　　❹ 爸爸　　❺ 姨妈

② (堂) ❶ 妈妈　　❷ 姨妈　　❸ 外婆　　❹ 堂妹　　❺ 表妹

③ (叔) ❶ 姨妈　　❷ 叔叔　　❸ 表哥　　❹ 表妹　　❺ 舅舅

④ (妈) ❶ 爸爸　　❷ 妈妈　　❸ 叔叔　　❹ 伯伯　　❺ 姑姑

⑤ (姐) ❶ 哥哥　　❷ 姐姐　　❸ 表哥　　❹ 堂哥　　❺ 堂妹

① 姨妈的儿子，小我两岁，他是我的_____ 八岁 。 *Biao Di*

② 叔叔的女儿，大我四岁，她是我的_____ 十岁x 。 *tangzie* 堂姐

③ 堂姐是伯伯的_____。 *Nü er*

④ 伯伯是奶奶的_____。 *er zi*

⑤ 弟弟和堂哥都是爷爷、奶奶的_____。 *Xuin zi*

⑥ 姨妈的女儿和我的妹妹都是外公、外婆的_____。 *Wai sui nüng*

⑦ 我是女的，舅舅是男的。我是外公的_____, *Jan Nauta*

舅舅是外公的_____。 *Jeroen* / *Hyeleco Nauta*

7 Go to *Exercise > Sentence Quiz* in your ⦿**Go300** to take the quiz. Choose the best two results.

		Accurate Spelling per Minute	Three Most Common Mistakes (Character)
Record 1	Date		
	Level	Time Elapsed	
Record 2	Date	Accurate Spelling per Minute	Three Most Common Mistakes (Character)
	Level	Time Elapsed	

TYPING RECORDS

8 Practice the strokes to write the characters.

wài	sūn	nǚ	gōng	pó
外	孙	女	公	婆

我是外公、外婆的 <u>外 孙 女</u> 。
　　　　　　　　　wài　sūn　nǚ

<u>外 公</u> 、 <u>外 婆</u> 爱我，我也爱他们。
wài　gōng　　wài　pó

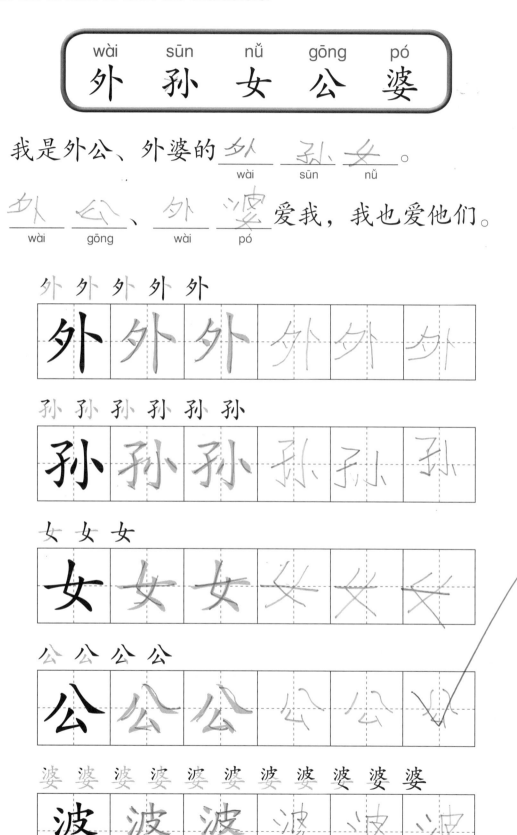

外 外 外 外 外

孙 孙 孙 孙 孙 孙

女 女 女

公 公 公 公

婆 婆 婆 婆 婆 婆 婆 婆 婆 婆

9 Check the boxes next to the sentences that accurately describe Ben and Tom's family.

Tom

A Ben是我的堂哥，他是我叔叔的儿子。

B Ben大我三岁，大我哥哥一岁。

C 我爷爷有两个儿子，没有女儿。

D 我外公有一个女儿和一个儿子。

E 我舅舅有两个女儿，她们都是我的表姐。

F Tom是我的堂弟，他是我伯伯的儿子。

G 我有一个妹妹，她叫Julia，小我四岁。

H 我爷爷有三个孙子和一个孙女。

I 我外公有两个女儿，没有儿子。

J 我有一个表哥，他大我两岁。

Ben

① ☒ Tom的姑姑有两个女儿。✓

② ☑ Tom有两个表姐、一个堂哥和一个堂妹。✓

③ ☒ Ben有两个表哥、两个堂弟和两个表姐。✓

④ ☒ Ben的爷爷也是Tom的爷爷。✗
他没有外孙，也没有外孙女。

⑤ ☑ Tom的爸爸就是Ben的伯伯，✓
Ben的爸爸就是Tom的叔叔。

TIP

Draw a family tree based on Tom and Ben's descriptions of their family. It will make it easier for you to complete the above task.

2

学校活动
School Activities

1 Fill in the table below.

English	Chinese	*Pinyin*
1	go to class	上课	shàng kè
2	school	学校	xúe xiào
3	join in/Participate	参加	cān jiā
4	rest	休息	xiū xi
5	music band	乐队	yuè dui
6	but/however	可是	kě shi
7	go home	回家	huí jiā
8	extra activities	课外活动	kè wài huó dòng

Somebody 送 Something 给 Somebody

Sb 送

2 Without changing the meaning of the original sentences, rewrite the sentences below by adding the word "给" to each of them.

给 gěi (gue)

Somebody (送 song) Somebody Something

ㄇ 马 马

1 我送妹妹一双鞋。
➡ 我送一双鞋给妹妹。

2 妈妈送弟弟一本书。
➡ 妈妈送一本书给弟弟。

3 外公送外婆一个杯子。
➡ 外公送一个杯子给外婆。

4 姨妈送表哥一台电脑。
➡ 姨妈送一台电脑给表哥。

3 Go to *Exercise > Sentence Quiz* in your Go 300 to take the quiz. Choose the best two results.

TYPING RECORDS		Date	Accurate Spelling per Minute	Three Most Common Mistakes (Character)
	Record 1			
		Level	Time Elapsed	
	Record 2	Date	Accurate Spelling per Minute	Three Most Common Mistakes (Character)
		Level	Time Elapsed	

4

Complete the two dialogues below with the words and phrases provided. Note that each word or phrase can only be used once in each dialogue.

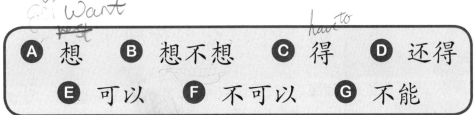

A 想　**B** 想不想　**C** 得　**D** 还得
E 可以　**F** 不可以　**G** 不能

① 😊：星期六你想不想参加乐队？

😊：我想参加，可是星期六我想不上打球，
不可以上中文课，我不能参加乐队。

😊：你可以不上中文课，来参加乐队吗？

😊：想，我爱中文课，我不能上中文课。

② 😊：星期六上午你想来我家吗？

😊：我想去，可是星期六上午，我还不得做功课，
不能写中文。我得去。

😊：下午我要去打球，你不能一起去？

😊：我想去，可是我要和哥哥
一起参加乐队。我可以去。

Go 300

In the CD, type the complete dialogues into the section "Exercise > Teacher's Assignment". Print it out and record down the time spent on the exercise.

Time Spent: _____

5 Using the pictures as clues, fill in B's replies to complete the conversations.

Ⓐ：下课回家你想休息吗？

Ⓑ：下课回家我想休息，可是
<u>我做功课</u>。

Ⓐ：你想去打球吗？

Ⓑ：我想去打球，<u>可是下雨</u>
_____。（可是）

Ⓐ：你想喝果汁吗？

Ⓑ：<u>我喝奶</u>_____
_____。（可是）

6 Go to *Exercise > Sentence Quiz* in your  to take the quiz. Choose the best two results.

<table>
<tr><td rowspan="4" style="writing-mode:vertical">TYPING RECORDS</td><td rowspan="2">Record
1</td><td>Date</td><td>Accurate Spelling
per Minute</td><td rowspan="2">Three Most Common Mistakes
(Character)</td></tr>
<tr><td>Level</td><td>Time Elapsed</td></tr>
<tr><td rowspan="2">Record
2</td><td>Date</td><td>Accurate Spelling
per Minute</td><td rowspan="2">Three Most Common Mistakes
(Character)</td></tr>
<tr><td>Level</td><td>Time Elapsed</td></tr>
</table>

7 Practice the strokes to write the characters.

xiào	huó	dòng	xiǎng	gěi
校	活	动	想	给

学 校 活 动 多，你 想 参加哪一个？

xiǎo　huó　dòng　　　　xiǎng

爸爸送了一双鞋 给 我，我 想 参加球队。

　　　　　　　gěi　　　　xiǎng

校 校 校 校 校 校 校 校 校 校

校	校	校	校	校	校

活 活 活 活 活 活 活 活 活

活	活	活	活	活	活

动 动 动 动 动 动

动	动	动	动	动	动

想 想 想 想 想 想 想 想 想 想 想

想	想	想	想	想	想

给 给 给 给 给 给 给 给

给	给	给	给	给	给

8 Rearrange the phrases to form a coherent sentence. In the boxes provided, write the corresponding letters in the correct order.

①
- **A** 有球队，有乐队，
- **B** 学校课外活动很多，
- **C** 我和同学一起参加乐队，
- **D** 上学真好玩！

➡ (D C A B)

②
- **A** 还得学电脑，
- **B** 可是我得参加球队，
- **C** 从早到晚都很忙。
- **D** 今天我的功课不多，

➡ (B C D A)

③
- **A** 爷爷对奶奶说：
- **B** 爷爷送了一台电脑给奶奶，
- **C** "没关系，我会教你用电脑的。"
- **D** 可是奶奶不会用。

➡ (A B C D)

④
- **A** 每个活动我都爱。
- **B** 每个活动都好玩，
- **C** 我除了要上课，
- **D** 还要参加很多活动，

➡ (D A B C)

用心做好
Try Your Best

1 Check the box next to the sentence that matches the picture. Then write down the *pinyin* for the underlined phrase in that sentence.

Picture	Sentence	Pinyin
①	☑ 哥哥的<u>成绩</u><u>好</u>。 ☐ 哥哥的<u>成绩</u>不好。	chéng jī hǎo
②	☑ 我的作业<u>写</u><u>完了</u>。 ☐ 我的作业<u>写</u>不完。	zuò yè xiě
③	☐ 他做功课<u>很用心</u>。 ☑ 他做功课<u>不用心</u>。	bù yong xīn
④	☑ 这个杯子<u>最大</u>。 ☐ 这个杯子<u>最小</u>。	zuì dà
⑤	☐ 我们<u>几点</u>大考？ ☑ 我们<u>什么时候</u>大考？ 6月18日	shen ma shí hou

2 Circle the phrases made up of two characters of the same tone. Indicate their tone by writing the phrases down in the appropriate blanks below.

First Tone : 开心

Second Tone : _____

Third Tone : 小考

Fourth Tone : 作业　重要 做事

3 Go to *Exercise > Sentence Quiz* in your to take the quiz. Choose the best two results.

		Accurate Spelling per Minute	Three Most Common Mistakes (Character)
Record 1	Date		
	Level	Time Elapsed	
Record 2	Date	Accurate Spelling per Minute	Three Most Common Mistakes (Character)
	Level	Time Elapsed	

4 Fill in the blanks with the words below.

a

A 忙不完	B 吃不完	C 写不完
D 写完了	E 考不完	F 考完了

① 今天作业很多，到晚上十点还是＿＿＿＿＿＿。

② 大考要考三天，到星期四就＿＿＿＿＿＿。

③ 奶奶做的饭菜太多，我们＿＿＿＿＿＿。

④ 大考小考很多，每天考试(kǎo shì)＿＿＿＿＿＿。

⑤ 弟弟的作业＿＿＿＿＿＿，他可以去打球了。

⑥ 妈妈要上班，还要做饭、洗衣服，

从早到晚＿＿＿＿＿＿。

b

A 开心	B 用心	C 小心

① 妈妈说："做功课要＿用心＿。"

② 路上车多，开车要＿＿＿＿。

③ 哥哥小考考得好，他很＿＿＿＿。

④ 成绩好坏不重要，＿＿＿＿做好最重要。

Go 300

In the CD, type the complete sentences into the section "Exercise > Teacher's Assignment". Print it out and record down the time spent on the exercise.

Time Spent: ＿＿＿＿＿＿

5 Using the pictures and the words as clues, complete the sentences below.

昨天的小考，Lily的成绩 最好
成绩 。（最……）

大关　小贵　小明

小明、大关和小贵三个人，＿＿＿＿
最高 。

（最高 / 最矮）

桌上有＿＿＿＿＿＿＿＿＿＿＿
＿＿＿＿＿＿＿＿＿＿＿ 。

（最想吃）

6 Go to *Exercise > Sentence Quiz* in your ⟨Go 300⟩ to take the quiz. Choose the best two results.

TYPING RECORDS		Date	Accurate Spelling per Minute	Three Most Common Mistakes (Character)
	Record 1			
		Level	Time Elapsed	
	Record 2	Date	Accurate Spelling per Minute	Three Most Common Mistakes (Character)
		Level	Time Elapsed	

7 Practice the strokes to write the characters.

考 完 交 作 最
kǎo wán jiāo zuò zuì

今天小考 考 完 了，明天要 交 作 业。
kǎo wán jiāo zuò

我要用心写 作 业，用心做好 最 重要。
zuò zuì

8a

Jeff's mother notices that Jeff (小明) is unhappy and she asks him why. Decide who might say the following sentences in the dialogue and fill in the blanks with either "妈妈" or "小明".

1. **妈妈**：上课用心学，不用怕(fear)大考和小考。

2. **小明**：每天用心上课、写作业，考好、考坏没关系。

3. **妈妈**：你为什么(why)不开心？

4. **小明**：可是我怕成绩不好。

5. **小明**：学校作业多，活动也多，大考、小考忙不完。我不想考大考。

6. **妈妈**：用心学，小心做，成绩好坏不重要。

7. **小明**：可是我怕考得不好。

8b

Rearrange the sentences above to create a logical dialogue and fill in the corresponding numbers in the correct order below.

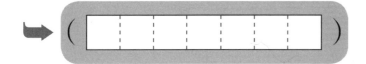

我生病了
I Am Sick

1 For each picture, write down the Chinese term, *pinyin* and English translation. The *pinyin* may be formed by combining the *pinyin* components below.

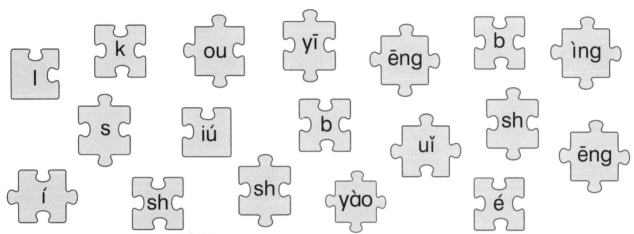

l · k · ou · yī · ēng · b · ìng · s · iú · b · uǐ · sh · ēng · í · sh · sh · yào · é

Picture	Chinese	*Pinyin*	English
①	流鼻水	liú bí shuǐ	running nose
②	咳嗽	ké sou	coughing
③	医生	yī shēng	doctor
④	药	yào	medicine
⑤	发烧	fā shāo	sick

2 Circle the correct phrase.

① 你的眼睛红红的，（怎么 / (什么)）了？

② 明天的小考要考（怎么 / (什么)）？

③ 你早饭吃了（(怎么) / 什么）？

④ 你生病了（(怎么) / 什么）不休息？

⑤ 你的小考（什么 / (怎么)）考不好？

⑥ 你（(什么) / 什么时候）可以出来玩？

⑦ **A**：你（怎么 / (什么时候)）可以回答我的问题？

   B：我明天下午可以回答你的问题。

3 Go to *Exercise > Sentence Quiz* in your 〔Go 300〕 to take the quiz. Choose the best two results.

		Accurate Spelling per Minute	Three Most Common Mistakes (Character)
Record 1	Date		
	Level	Time Elapsed	
Record 2	Date	Accurate Spelling per Minute	Three Most Common Mistakes (Character)
	Level	Time Elapsed	

4 Fill in the blanks with either "出来" or "出去".

小明：小贵，<u>出来</u>！我们一起去

打球，好不好？

小贵：等一等，我穿好鞋子就<u>出来</u>。

小明：你哥哥在家吗？他要不要一起去

打球？

小贵：我哥哥不在家，他<u>出去</u>了。

Go 300

In the CD, type the complete dialogue into the section "Exercise > Teacher's Assignment". Print it out and record down the time spent on the exercise.

Time Spent: _____

5 Using the clues given, complete the dialogue below.

😐：你怎么了？

🌑：_____。（咳嗽 / 真难过）

😐：_____？（几天）

🌑：我咳嗽咳了五天了。

😐：你看医生了吗？

🌑：_____。

医生要我吃药，他说不吃药，_____。

6 Pick the odd one out.

① (3) **❶** 吃药   **❷** 医生   **❸** 堂哥   **❹** 流鼻水

② (3) **❶** 怎么   **❷** 什么   **❸** 不会   **❹** 能不能

③ (4) **❶** 休息   **❷** 吃药   **❸** 喝水   **❹** 流鼻水

④ (4) **❶** 幸福   **❷** 难过   **❸** 辛苦   **❹** 不开心

7 Rewrite the following sentences in the sentence structure shown in **①**.

① 妹妹的小考考得真好。
➡ 妹妹（考）小考，（考）得真好。

② 妈妈的菜做得真好吃。
➡ 妈妈做菜，_____。

8 Go to *Exercise > Sentence Quiz* in your [Go 300] to take the quiz. Choose the best two results.

		Date	Accurate Spelling per Minute	Three Most Common Mistakes (Character)
TYPING RECORDS	**Record 1**			
		Level	Time Elapsed	
	Record 2	Date	Accurate Spelling per Minute	Three Most Common Mistakes (Character)
		Level	Time Elapsed	

9 Practice the strokes to write the characters.

liú	shuǐ	nán	guò	bìng
流	水	难	过	病

我 <u>流</u> 鼻 <u>水</u> 了，真 <u>难</u> <u>过</u>。
　　liú　　　shuǐ　　　　　nán　　guò

我 生 <u>病</u> 了，我 要 去 看 医 生。
　　　bìng

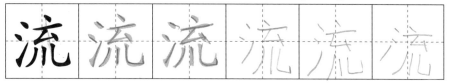

流 流 流 流 流 流 流 流 流 流

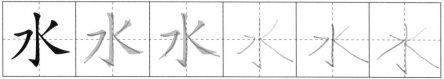

水 水 水 水

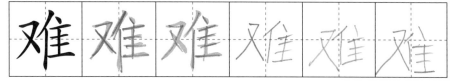

难 难 难 难 难 难 难 难 难 难

过 过 过 过 过 过

病 病 病 病 病 病 病 病 病

10a

Using the pictures as clues, complete the following sentences.

医生除了要我＿＿＿＿＿＿＿＿＿＿＿

＿＿＿＿＿＿＿＿，还要＿＿＿＿＿＿＿。

昨天天气不好，我＿＿＿＿＿＿了。

妈妈说："生病了，＿＿＿＿＿＿＿＿＿

＿＿＿＿＿＿＿＿＿＿＿＿＿＿。"

医生问我怎么了？我说："＿＿＿＿＿

＿＿＿＿＿＿＿＿＿＿＿＿＿＿。"

10b

Rearrange the above scenarios in the order which they occurred and fill in the corresponding numbers in the correct order below.

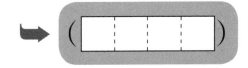

家在哪里?
Where Is Your Home?

1 Fill in the table with the *pinyin* that matches each picture and write the corresponding Chinese words out.

> **A** shì chǎng **B** tíng chē chǎng **C** qiú chǎng
>
> **D** fàn guǎn **E** tú shū guǎn **F** yī yuàn

Picture	*Pinyin*	Chinese
①		
②		
③		
④		
⑤		

2 Fill in the blanks according to the diagram below.

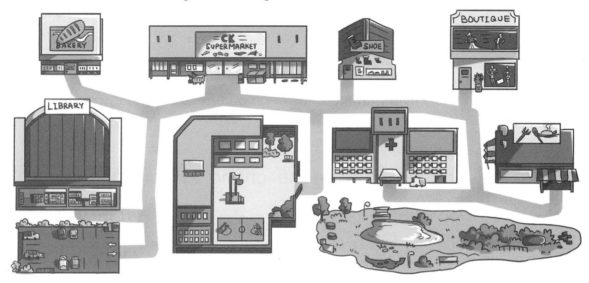

① 学校左边有_____。

② 学校对面有_____。

③ _____在学校后面。

④ _____在医院左边。

⑤ 停车场在图书馆_____。

3 Go to *Exercise > Sentence Quiz* in your [Go 300] to take the quiz. Choose the best two results.

TYPING RECORDS		Date	Accurate Spelling per Minute	Three Most Common Mistakes (Character)
	Record 1			
		Level	Time Elapsed	
	Record 2	Date	Accurate Spelling per Minute	Three Most Common Mistakes (Character)
		Level	Time Elapsed	

4

Check the box next to the appropriate sentence to complete each dialogue. You may check more than one box for each question.

1 **A**：请问市场在哪里？

B：
- ☐ 除了市场，还有图书馆和学校。
- ☐ 市场在医院附近。
- ☐ 市场就在我家对面。

2 **A**：
- ☐ 请问去图书馆怎么走？
- ☐ 请问去学校怎么走？
- ☐ 你家附近有图书馆吗？

B：从学校出来向左转，再向前走就到了。

3 **A**：你家附近有医院吗？

B：
- ☐ 没有，我家附近有图书馆。
- ☐ 我家附近有医院，还有图书馆。
- ☐ 医院就在我家对面。

4 **A**：学校离医院近吗？

B：
- ☐ 很近，医院就在我家对面。
- ☐ 很近，从学校到医院，走五分钟就到了。
- ☐ 学校附近没有医院。

5 Using the words provided, translate the following sentences into Chinese following the sentence structure shown in ❶.

爷爷	奶奶
舅舅	姑姑
表哥	妹妹
学生	我

学校	图书馆
市场	停车场
医院	球场
饭馆	草地

开车	看病
看书	打球
买菜	停车
上课	吃饭

❶ Students go to school to study.

学生去学校上课。

❷ My uncle parks in the parking lot.

_____

❸ My grandfather and I eat in the restaurant.

_____

❹ My cousin sees a doctor in the hospital.

_____

6 Go to *Exercise > Sentence Quiz* in your [Go 300] to take the quiz. Choose the best two results.

TYPING RECORDS

		Date	Accurate Spelling per Minute	Three Most Common Mistakes (Character)
Record 1				
		Level	Time Elapsed	
Record 2		Date	Accurate Spelling per Minute	Three Most Common Mistakes (Character)
		Level	Time Elapsed	

7 Practice the strokes to write the characters.

zhù	xiàng	zhuǎn	tú	guǎn
住	向	转	图	馆

我____在学校对面。从我家____前走，
    zhù   xiàng

再____右____，就到____书____了。
  xiàng   zhuǎn   tú   guǎn

住 住 住 住 住 住 住

住 住 住

向 向 向 向 向 向

向 向 向

转 转 转 转 转 转 转 转

转 转 转

图 图 图 图 图 图 图 图

图 图 图

馆 馆 馆 馆 馆 馆 馆 馆 馆 馆 馆

馆 馆 馆

8 Answer the questions according to the diagram below.

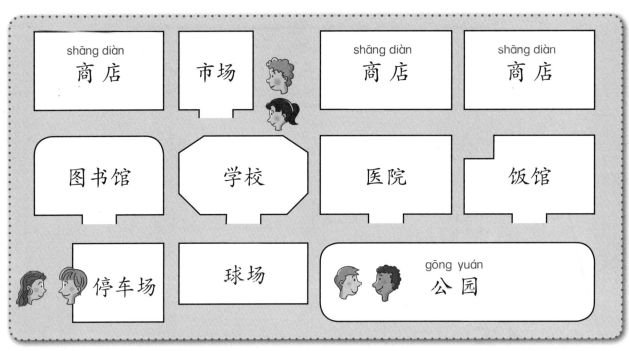

: 请问饭馆在哪里？

: 饭馆在＿＿＿＿＿＿＿＿＿＿＿＿＿＿＿＿＿＿＿。（医院）

: 请问去饭馆怎么走？

: ＿＿＿＿＿＿＿＿＿＿＿＿＿＿＿＿＿＿＿＿＿。

: 请问去停车场怎么走？

: ＿＿＿＿＿＿＿＿＿＿＿＿＿＿＿＿＿＿＿＿＿。

: 停车场离市场近吗？

: ＿＿＿＿＿＿＿＿＿＿＿＿＿＿＿＿＿＿＿＿＿。

（近／走十分钟）

REVIEW 1

1. In the right column, circle the phrases which are in the same tone as the phrase in the left column.

1	附近	用心	(作业)	(做事)	市场
2	生病	活动	看书	(出去)	(方便)
3	成绩	(堂哥)	球队	参加	时候
4	什么	名字	市场	鞋子	难过
5	咳嗽	伯伯	果汁	回家	球队
6	休息	学校	眼睛	医生	衣服
7	市场	球场	饭馆	绿灯	下午
8	可是	外孙	还得	好坏	很大

2 Circle the extra word in each of the following sentences.

① 从学校出来，向左转就可以到去图书馆了。

② 我生病了，鼻子水流不停。

③ 我和堂妹同样姓，我们都姓王。

④ 这个问题怎么了回答？

⑤ 学校有课外活动多，我参加乐队，真好玩！

3 Fill in the blanks with the correct punctuation (， ！ 。 ？ ： " ").

① 老师问我们□□去图书馆怎么走□□

② 课外活动我都爱□除了参加球队□我还参加乐队□

③ 你怎么了□咳嗽咳个不停□

④ □忙□和□忘□这两个字都有□心□□

⑤ 他是我的爷爷□也是堂姐的爷爷□
   我们都是一家人□

4a

Using the words below, form a sentence starting with "星" and ending with "了". Connect these words with a continuous line.

星	期	动	课	参	家	出	去	了
校	六	加	只	停	在	能	过	妹
活	爷	姑	考	完	咳	不	停	成
功	爷	姑	生	医	院	出	不	绩
附	想	和	馆	可	是	住	咳	嗽
交	近	我	书	书	我	院	难	咳
流	水	去	图	看	生	病	了	我

4b

From the sentence formed above, pick out the characters whose *pinyin* end with "u" or "e" and classify them in the spaces below.

Characters with the final "u":

Characters with the final "e":

5

Rewrite the following sentences by appropriately adding the word "最" to express the superlative.

① 妹妹写字很好看。

_____

② 哥哥的成绩很好。

_____

③ 用心做事很重要。

_____

6 Fill in the blanks with the words below.

a Ⓐ 忙不忙   Ⓑ 想不想   Ⓒ 好不好   Ⓓ 近不近

❶ 外公问我_____去舅舅家？

❷ 星期天我们去图书馆看书，_____？

❸ 从市场到停车场_____？

b Ⓐ 用不用心   Ⓑ 重不重要
    Ⓒ 好不好吃   Ⓓ 幸不幸福

❶ 小明问我，今天的活动_____？

❷ 爸爸做的早饭_____？

❸ 你上课_____？

7 Translate the following sentences into English.

❶ 我送奶奶一本书。

_____

❷ 我送两支笔给哥哥。

_____

8 The following diagram is a map of the area around Jeff's (小明) house. The numbers represent the time taken to travel between two points (in minutes). With the description below, decipher what A, B, C, D, and E are and answer the questions that follow.

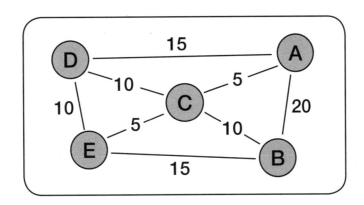

➡ 小明家附近有市场、学校、医院和图书馆。

➡ 从小明家到学校，走五分钟就到了。

➡ 从学校到图书馆很近，走五分钟就到了。

➡ 从小明家到医院要走十五分钟。

➡ 从小明家到市场要走十分钟。

➡ 从学校到医院要走十分钟。

1 What do the letters represent on the map? Write the letters next to the corresponding locations below.

☐ 图书馆　　☐ 市场

☐ 小明家　　☐ 医院

☐ 学校

2 Complete this sentence.

医院和_____最近，走_____分钟就到了。

9 Rearrange the following sentences to form a coherent text by labelling them in order using letters "a" to "j".

1. ☐ 到了下午四点，我下课了，

2. ☐ 爷爷每天都会问我："在学校开心吗？"

3. ⓐ 爷爷和我们住在一起，

4. ☐ 爷爷开车来接我回家，

5. ☐ 每天早上爷爷送我去上学，

6. ☐ 学校附近有图书馆，

7. ☐ 从我家到学校，开车要十五分钟。

8. ☐ 我去学校上课，爷爷就去图书馆看书。

9. ☐ 我对爷爷说："今天我学会了很多中文字，很开心。"

10. ☐ 爷爷说，我开心，他也很开心。

Go 300
In the CD, type the rearranged text into the section "Exercise > Teacher's Assignment". Print it out and record down the time spent on the exercise.

Time Spent: _____

1 For each word or phrase, write down its Chinese term and *pinyin*.

English	Chinese	*Pinyin*
① beautiful	美丽	měi lì
② quarrel	吵架	chǎo jià
③ scold others	骂人	mà ren
④ mood	心情	xīn qíng
⑤ self	自己	zì jǐ
⑥ because		
⑦ angry	生气	shēng qì
⑧ sad	难过	nán guò

don't have to do

2

For each picture, indicate the mood of the scenario by writing down either "开心" or "难过" in the rectangle beside the picture. Draw "☺" in the circle at the bottom of the picture which you feel "最开心" about, and "☹" in the one you feel "最难过" about.

3

Go to *Exercise > Sentence Quiz* in your [Go 300] to take the quiz. Choose the best two results.

TYPING RECORDS		Date	Accurate Spelling per Minute	Three Most Common Mistakes (Character)
	Record 1			
		Level	Time Elapsed	
	Record 2	Date	Accurate Spelling per Minute	Three Most Common Mistakes (Character)
		Level	Time Elapsed	

4

Fill in the blanks with the words below to form appropriate phrases. Each word can only be used once.

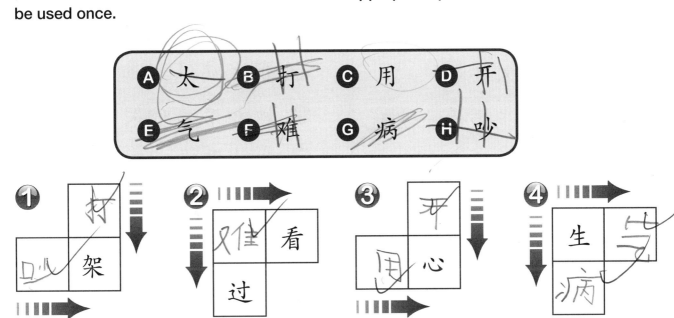

| A 太 | B 打 | C 用 | D 开 |
| E 气 | F 难 | G 病 | H 吵 |

① 打 吵 架

② 难 看 过

③ 开 用 心

④ 生 气 病

5

Complete the following sentences using the phrases formed in Question 4.

① 弟弟不_____，因为他和哥哥_____了。

② 因为弟弟和妹妹_____，所以妈妈很_____。

③ 我__生病__了，不能去上学。

④ 爸爸骂哥哥做事不__生气__。

⑤ 我病好了，可以出去玩了，我很__开心__。

⑥ 心情不好，看什么都__生气__。

⑦ 他的大考考不好，很__难过__。

29.09.2013

6 Mix and match sentences from the two boxes to form sentences that fit into the sentence structure "因为……，所以……".

A 她很不开心

B 我不能和你出去玩

C 昨天我没去上学

D 妈妈很生气

E 我生病了，鼻水流不停

F 她和弟弟吵架了

G 我昨天没回家

H 他心情不好

I 我今天得去看病

❶ 因为 [E] ，所以 [C] 。 ✓

❷ 因为 [D] ，所以 [H] 。 ✓

❸ 因为她很不开心，所以 I

❹ 因为 G 所以 A ✓

7 Go to *Exercise > Sentence Quiz* in your [Go 300] to take the quiz. Choose the best two results.

TYPING RECORDS		Date	Accurate Spelling per Minute	Three Most Common Mistakes (Character)
	Record 1			
		Level	Time Elapsed	
		Date	Accurate Spelling per Minute	Three Most Common Mistakes (Character)
	Record 2			
		Level	Time Elapsed	

8 Practice the strokes to write the characters.

yīn	wèi	měi	qíng	chǎo
因	为	美	情	吵

因 为 ____ 春天到了，所以花开得很 美 ____ 丽。
  yīn wèi   měi

他的心 情 ____ 不好，因为他和弟弟 吵 ____ 架了。
     qíng   chǎo

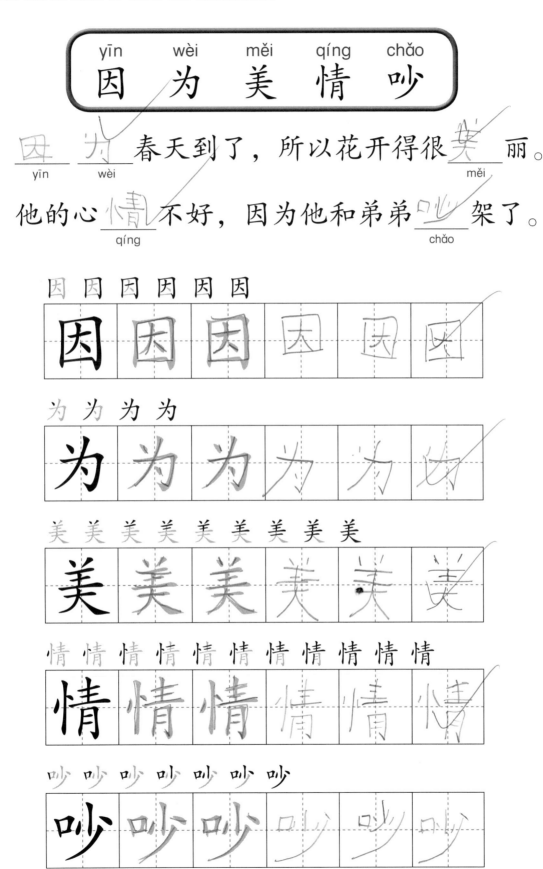

因 因 因 因 因 因

| 因 | 因 | 因 | 因 | 因 | 因 |

为 为 为 为

| 为 | 为 | 为 | 为 | 为 | 为 |

美 美 美 美 美 美 美 美 美

| 美 | 美 | 美 | 美 | 美 | 美 |

情 情 情 情 情 情 情 情 情 情

| 情 | 情 | 情 | 情 | 情 | 情 |

吵 吵 吵 吵 吵 吵 吵

| 吵 | 吵 | 吵 | 吵 | 吵 | 吵 |

9 Read the following passage. Check the boxes next to the sentences that accurately describe the content of the passage.

> 昨天我生病了，没去学校。晚上小明打电话找我，他对我说："小贵，生病了要多休息，你不会的功课，我可以教你。"
>
> 今天我病好了，我可以去上学了，我很开心。

❶ ☑ 小明昨天生病了，他没去上学。✗

❷ ☑ 小明打电话找小贵。✓

❸ ☑ 小贵生病了，二月十七日没去上学。✗

❹ ☒ 小明说功课太多，他做不完。✓

❺ ☐ 小明可以教小贵做功课。

❻ ☑ 二月十八日，小贵去上学了。✓

❼ ☐ 小贵要小明教他做功课。

❽ ☐ 小贵打电话找小明，问今天的功课。

Read the text carefully.

2013. 10. 13.

Go 300
In the CD, type the passage into the section "Exercise > Teacher's Assignment". Print it out and record down the time spent on the exercise.

Time Spent: _____

我看球赛
Watching a Ball Game

1 Write down the word of each *pinyin*. Then check the box next to the matching picture.

Pinyin	Chinese	Picture
① lán qiú		☐ ☐
② bàng qiú		☐ ☐
③ jǐn zhāng		☐ ☐
④ jīng cǎi		☐ ☐
⑤ mǎi piào		☐ ☐
⑥ hóng duì shū le		☐ ☐

2 Circle the correct answer and write it down.

1 _____ 我今天看了一场（晴／精）彩的球赛。

2 _____ 爸爸说（运／这）动很重要。

3 _____ 学校有很多（活／话）动，你要参加哪一个?

4 _____ 表弟爱和我们（北一北／比一比），看谁高。

5 _____ 弟弟喜（欢／观）和同学一起打棒球。

6 _____ 哥哥大考考得好，所以他心（情／请）很好。

7 _____ 今天的比赛很重要，可是我（输／转）了。

8 _____ 妹妹想（白／自）己去上学，不要妈妈送她
去学校。

3 Go to *Exercise > Sentence Quiz* in your Go 300 to take the quiz. Choose the best two results.

TYPING RECORDS		Date	Accurate Spelling per Minute	Three Most Common Mistakes (Character)
	Record 1			
		Level	Time Elapsed	
	Record 2	Date	Accurate Spelling per Minute	Three Most Common Mistakes (Character)
		Level	Time Elapsed	

4 Check the box next to the sentence that accurately describes the picture.

1

- ☐ 大关和小明比赛，他们两个打得一样好。
- ☐ 大关赢小明两分。
- ☐ 小明打得比大关好。

2

- ☐ 弟弟想看乒乓球比赛。
- ☐ 哥哥不想看篮球比赛。
- ☐ 弟弟生气了，因为他们都想看棒球比赛。

3

- ☐ 很多人想参加球队。
- ☐ 很多人想看球赛。
- ☐ 很多人想买票看棒球比赛。

4

	1	2	3	4	5	6	7	8	9
白队	0	0	0	1	0	0	0	0	2
蓝队	1	0	0	1	2	3	0	0	0

- ☐ 三比七，白队赢了。
- ☐ 白队输蓝队三分。
- ☐ 蓝队赢了，蓝队赢了四分。

Go 300

In the CD, type the correct sentences into the section "Exercise > Teacher's Assignment". Print it out and record down the time spent on the exercise.

Time Spent: _____

5 Using the pictures and words as clues, describe the differences between the two subjects in each picture.

①

	1	2	3	4	5	6	7	8	9
红队	0	0	1	0	0	2	0	0	0
白队	0	0	0	0	3	0	1	0	-

三＿＿＿＿＿＿四，白队＿＿＿＿＿＿，

白队＿＿＿＿＿红队一分。

②

\$2.49 MILK \$4.49 Fruit Juice

＿＿＿＿＿＿＿＿＿＿＿两块钱。

（便宜）

③

Michael
15 Years Old

Issac
11 Years Old

＿＿＿＿＿＿＿＿＿＿＿＿＿＿＿＿

＿＿＿＿＿＿＿＿＿＿＿＿＿＿＿＿

（小 / 岁）

6 Go to *Exercise > Sentence Quiz* in your to take the quiz. Choose the best two results.

		Date	Accurate Spelling per Minute	Three Most Common Mistakes (Character)
Record 1				
		Level	Time Elapsed	
		Date	Accurate Spelling per Minute	Three Most Common Mistakes (Character)
Record 2				
		Level	Time Elapsed	

7 Practice the strokes to write the characters.

jīng	cǎi	bǐ	piào	yùn
精	彩	比	票	运

明天有一场＿＿＿＿＿的棒球＿＿赛，我想

<u>jīng</u>　　<u>cǎi</u>　　　<u>bǐ</u>

买＿＿去看球赛。棒球是我最喜欢的＿＿动。

<u>piào</u>　　　　　　　　　　　<u>yùn</u>

精 精 精 精 精 精 精 精 精 精 精 精 精

精	精	精	精	精	精

彩 彩 彩 彩 彩 彩 彩 彩 彩 彩 彩

彩	彩	彩	彩	彩	彩

比 比 比 比

比	比	比	比	比	比

票 票 票 票 票 票 票 票 票 票 票

票	票	票	票	票	票

运 运 运 运 运 运 运

运	运	运	运	运	运

8 The following text is a report on a baseball game. Read the report and answer the questions that follow.

Second victorious game for Reds as it beat Whites 8:2

Yesterday, the Reds played against the Whites in the fourth game of the best-of-five tournament. The game started with the Reds batting first. In the first half of the sixth inning, the Reds broke the outstanding tie with their score of eight points, and eventually clinched the victory with a stunning score of eight to two against the defending champions for two consecutive games.

The Reds delivered an outstanding performance paralleled by no other. Within the first six innings, the first pitcher for the Reds, Mike, had struck out seven batters of the Whites. In the sixth inning, the Reds went all out with Vince hitting home run with all bases loaded, obtaining four points for his team. Subsequently, an error in the Whites' defense contributed another four points to the Reds. The fate of the Whites did not improve in the last three innings, even though the team obtained a point each in the seventh and ninth inning. It was just not enough to turn the tables around, leading to their eventual loss.

Supporters of the Reds claimed unanimously that this was the most exciting game they had ever seen. The coach has also expressed his full confidence in the team's abilities to win the next game the following week. The two teams have competed in four out of five games, with both of them deadlocked in their score of two games each. The deciding game will take place next Friday.

8a Complete the score chart below according to the report. Fill in the teams' names in Chinese.

Team	1	2	3	4	5	6	7	8	9	Total
	0	0	0	0	0	8				
	0	0	0	0	0	0				

8b Answer the following questions.

① 两队的比分(score)是多少？

两队的比分是＿＿＿＿＿＿＿＿＿＿＿＿＿＿＿＿。

② 哪一个队赢了比赛？赢了几分？

＿＿＿＿＿＿＿＿＿＿＿＿＿＿＿＿＿＿＿＿＿

③ 红队赢了几场比赛？他们还有几场比赛？

＿＿＿＿＿＿＿＿＿＿＿＿＿＿＿＿＿＿＿＿＿

我的爱好
My Hobbies

1 Fill in the first column with the words provided. Then write down the *pinyin* and English translation for each answer.

A 歌 **B** 音乐 **C** 游戏 **D** 书	
E 字 **F** 功课 **G** 作业 **H** 舞	

	Chinese	*Pinyin*	English
1	跳_____		
2	交_____		
3	写_____		write words
4	唱_____		
5	做_____	zuò gōng kè	
6	玩_____		
7	看_____		
8	听_____		

2 Match each picture to the sentence that accurately describes it.

A 妹妹一边听音乐，一边唱歌。

B 堂妹一边看书，一边唱歌。

C 姐姐一边做饭，一边看电视。

D 我喜欢看书，也喜欢唱歌。

3 Go to *Exercise > Sentence Quiz* in your **Go 300** to take the quiz. Choose the best two results.

TYPING RECORDS		Date	Accurate Spelling per Minute	Three Most Common Mistakes (Character)
	Record 1			
		Level	Time Elapsed	
	Record 2	Date	Accurate Spelling per Minute	Three Most Common Mistakes (Character)
		Level	Time Elapsed	

4a ① , ② , and ③ are parts of a dialogue between A and B. Choose the appropriate replies for B by checking the boxes next to your choice.

① **A**：你喜欢看书，还是运动？

B：
- ☐ 我喜欢运动，我最喜欢看书。
- ☐ 我喜欢跳舞，也喜欢运动。
- ☐ 我喜欢看书，也喜欢运动。

② **A**：你常常去看球赛吗？

B：
- ☐ 不，我常常去看球赛。
- ☐ 我很少去看。我喜欢看球赛，可是票太贵了。
- ☐ 我有时去打球，有时去运动。

③ **A**：你喜欢做什么运动？

B：
- ☐ 我喜欢运动，可是我不喜欢看球赛。
- ☐ 我什么运动都不喜欢。
- ☐ 我喜欢打棒球，也喜欢看球赛。

4b Arrange ① , ② , and ③ in the order which they occur in the dialogue, and write down the corresponding numbers in the correct order below.

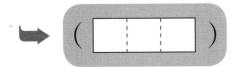

5 Decipher the common pattern in ① to ③ to expand the phrases and sentences.

① ＿＿＿＿＿ ▸ 看<u>什么</u>书？ ▸ <u>你想</u>看什么书？

② 跳舞 ▸ 跳＿＿＿＿＿舞？ ▸ 你想＿＿＿＿＿？

③ 唱歌 ▸ ＿＿＿＿＿＿＿ ▸ ＿＿＿＿＿＿＿

6 Rearrange the phrases to form a coherent sentence and write down the corresponding numbers in the correct order.

①
❶ 姐姐　❷ 她常常　❸ 一起唱歌　❹ 和朋友　❺ 喜欢唱歌

▸ (＿｜＿｜＿，＿｜＿｜＿｜＿。)

②
❶ 很少　❷ 我们　❸ 舅舅　❹ 都很想他　❺ 回家

▸ (＿｜＿｜＿，＿｜＿｜＿。)

7 Go to *Exercise > Sentence Quiz* in your 〔Go 300〕 to take the quiz. Choose the best two results.

TYPING RECORDS

		Date	Accurate Spelling per Minute	Three Most Common Mistakes (Character)
Record 1				
		Level	Time Elapsed	
Record 2		Date	Accurate Spelling per Minute	Three Most Common Mistakes (Character)
		Level	Time Elapsed	

8 Practice the strokes to write the characters.

chàng	gē	cháng	péng	yǒu
唱	歌	常	朋	友

姐姐喜欢＿＿＿ ＿＿＿，她＿＿＿ ＿＿＿和
　　　　　　chàng　　gē　　　　　cháng　cháng

＿＿＿ ＿＿＿一起唱歌。
péng　　you

唱 唱 唱 唱 唱 唱 唱 唱 唱 唱

| 唱 | 唱 | 唱 | | | |

歌 歌 歌 歌 歌 歌 歌 歌 歌 歌 歌 歌 歌 歌

| 歌 | 歌 | 歌 | | | |

常 常 常 常 常 常 常 常 常 常 常

| 常 | 常 | 常 | | | |

朋 朋 朋 朋 朋 朋 朋 朋

| 朋 | 朋 | 朋 | | | |

友 友 友 友

| 友 | 友 | 友 | | | |

The following table shows the co-curricular activities schedule for 小明, 小贵, and 大关. Study it and answer the questions that follow.

	星期日	星期一	星期二	星期三	星期四	星期五	星期六
小明	乐队	乐队			棒球		棒球
小贵	棒球	乐队		棒球			棒球
大关				棒球	棒球		棒球

① 他们喜欢打什么球？

_____

② 大关一个星期打几次球？星期四他和谁一起打球？

_____

③ 小贵每天打球吗？（有时……，有时……）

_____

④ 小贵一个星期打360分钟的球，请问小贵每次都打几个小时的球？ (The duration of each game is the same.)

_____

电视节目
Television Programs

1 Check the box next to the sentence that matches the picture. Then write down the *pinyin* for the underlined word in that sentence.

Picture	Sentence	*Pinyin*
1	☐ 妹妹喜欢看<u>卡通</u>。 ☐ 妹妹喜欢看<u>电影</u>。	
2	☐ <u>电视节目</u>很好看。 ☐ <u>电影</u>很好看。	
3	☐ 哥哥一回家就打开<u>电视</u>。 ☐ 哥哥一回家就看<u>节目表</u>。	
4	☐ 奶奶会说<u>英文</u>。 ☐ 奶奶会说<u>中文</u>。	
5	☐ 弟弟<u>自己</u>看<u>电视</u>。 ☐ 弟弟<u>自己</u>选<u>电视节目</u>。	

Search for phrases hidden in the puzzle and circle them.

卡	通	打	开	自
加	种	英	心	己
电	视	选	节	目
影	机	新	文	唱
跳	舞	闻	久	歌

2b

Use the phrases to complete the sentences below.

妹妹最喜欢看跳舞的＿＿＿＿＿＿，

因为她的爱好是＿＿＿＿＿＿。

哥哥一回家就＿＿＿＿＿＿，

他每天都要看＿＿＿＿＿＿。

3

Go to *Exercise > Sentence Quiz* in your to take the quiz. Choose the best two results.

		Date	Accurate Spelling per Minute	Three Most Common Mistakes (Character)
Record 1				
	Level		Time Elapsed	
		Date	Accurate Spelling per Minute	Three Most Common Mistakes (Character)
Record 2				
	Level		Time Elapsed	

TYPING RECORDS

4

Complete the passage below with the phrases provided.

A 一起看卡通

B 一起看电视

C 家人看什么节目

D 喜欢看电影

E 喜欢看唱歌的节目

F 喜欢看新闻

G 每一种节目我都爱

每天晚上，我们全家人喜欢＿＿＿＿＿＿＿＿＿＿＿＿。

爸爸＿＿＿＿＿＿＿＿，他说看新闻可以知道*很多事；

妈妈＿＿＿＿＿＿＿＿＿＿＿，她说歌星*唱的歌真好听；

哥哥＿＿＿＿＿＿＿＿＿，他说电影真精彩；我喜欢和

家人一起看电视，＿＿＿＿＿＿＿＿＿＿，我就看什么节

目，我什么节目都喜欢。

*知道 know
*歌星 singer

5 Circle the extra word in each of the following sentences.

① 卡通、电影和加新闻我都喜欢。

② 你就想看什么电影？

③ 老师要我交完了作业再去玩。

④ 今天上课上了很久，所以我还没去回家吃饭。

⑤ 电视节目很精彩，可是不要去看太久。

⑥ 我喜欢听哥哥唱歌，哥哥唱歌真很好听。

⑦ 堂姐找了太很久，还是找不到她的帽子。

⑧ 你一看什么电影，我就看什么电影。

> **Go 300**
> In the CD, type the correct sentences into the section "Exercise > Teacher's Assignment". Print it out and record down the time spent on the exercise.
> Time Spent: _____

6 Go to *Exercise > Sentence Quiz* in your **Go 300** to take the quiz. Choose the best two results.

TYPING RECORDS

		Date	Accurate Spelling per Minute	Three Most Common Mistakes (Character)
Record 1				
	Level	Time Elapsed		
		Date	Accurate Spelling per Minute	Three Most Common Mistakes (Character)
Record 2				
	Level	Time Elapsed		

7 Practice the strokes to write the characters.

shì	mù	xīn	yīng	tōng
视	目	新	英	通

每天都有好看的电＿＿＿节＿＿＿。
　　　　　　　　　　shì　　　 mù

我爱看＿＿＿闻，妹妹喜欢看＿＿＿文卡＿＿＿。
　　　　xīn　　　　　　　　　　yīng　　　　tōng

视 视 视 视 视 视 视 视

视	视	视			

目 目 目 目 目

目	目	目			

新 新 新 新 新 新 新 新 新 新 新 新

新	新	新			

英 英 英 英 英 英 英 英

英	英	英			

通 通 通 通 通 通 通 通 通 通

通	通	通			

8 The following is a statistical summary of TV viewership on a typical Sunday in Go Town, where 1000 people reside. Study it and answer the questions that follow.

A Population by Age

Age	No. of People
0-20	194
20-40	287
40-60	235
60-80	201
above 80	83

B Male–Female Proportion of TV Viewers

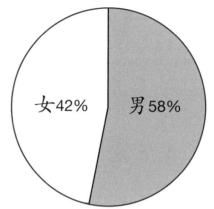

C TV Viewership at Various Time Slots

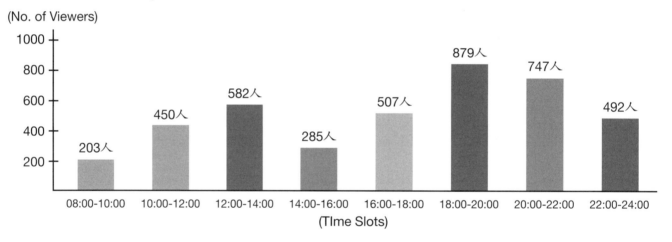

D TV Viewership by Category of Shows in the Morning and Afternoon

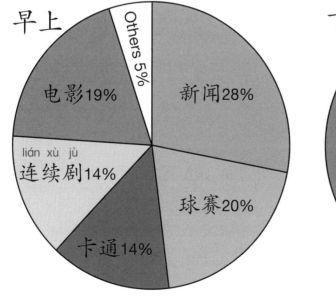

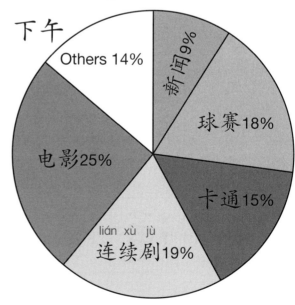

8a Check the boxes next to the sentences that accurately describe TV viewership in Go Town.

1. ☐ 星期日在家看电视的女生比男生多。

2. ☐ 下午两点到四点看电视的人比下午四点到六点的多。

3. ☐ 早上看新闻的人最少。

4. ☐ 这个小镇(town)二十到四十岁的人最多。
   xiǎo zhèn

5. ☐ 早上看卡通和看连续剧的人一样多。
   lián xù jù

6. ☐ 下午看新闻的人比看球赛的少。

7. ☐ 下午看电影的人比看卡通的多。

8b Answer the following questions in complete sentence in Chinese.

1. 几点看电视节目的人最少？

   _____

2. 几点看电视节目的人最多？

   _____

3. 晚上九点看电视的人比早上九点多多少人？

   _____

4. 下午看什么节目的人最多？

   _____

今天天气
The Weather Today

1 Fill in the blanks with the correct Chinese words and *pinyin*.

今天是 晴天 ，天是蓝色的，＿＿＿＿＿很大，
<u>tài yáng</u>

天气很 热 。大树喜欢＿＿＿＿＿，大树会看着
<u>tài yáng</u>

＿＿＿＿＿ 笑 ；大树也喜欢 下雨 ，大树可以
<u>yáng guāng</u>

＿＿＿＿＿嘴喝水。
<u>zhāng zhe</u>

我喜欢晴天，不喜欢 雨天 。下雨，我就

不能＿＿＿＿＿玩了。
<u>chū qù</u>

你喜欢什么天气？

2 Fill in the blanks with the words below.

A 唱着	**B** 喝着	**C** 做着	**D** 张着	**E** 听着
F 开着	**G** 跳着	**H** 看着	**I** 下着	**J** 说着

① 小明_____嘴唱歌。

② 妈妈_____我说："你做得真好！"

③ 妹妹_____音乐写作业，妈妈说她不用心。

④ 外面_____雨，我们不能出去玩了。

⑤ 姐姐送我去上学，她_____车，

我_____歌，我们都很开心。

> **Go 300**
>
> In the CD, type the complete sentences into the section "Exercise > Teacher's Assignment". Print it out and record down the time spent on the exercise.
>
> Time Spent: _____

3 Go to *Exercise > Sentence Quiz* in your **Go 300** to take the quiz. Choose the best two results.

TYPING RECORDS		Date	Accurate Spelling per Minute	Three Most Common Mistakes (Character)
	Record 1			
		Level	Time Elapsed	
	Record 2	Date	Accurate Spelling per Minute	Three Most Common Mistakes (Character)
		Level	Time Elapsed	

Look at the following dialogues between the characters. Check the boxes next to the sentences that accurately describe the content of each dialogue. You may check more than one box for each dialogue.

☐ 明天是晴天。

☐ 明天会下雨。

☐ 明天大关会去打球。

☐ 明天天气好，大关就会去打球。

☐ Sarah赢了！

☐ Luke的中文书比Sarah少。

☐ Luke的哥哥送了两本书给他。

5 Write ✓ in the box next to the sentence if it is logical, and write ✗ if it is not logical. Circle the error and write the corrected sentence in the space provided.

① ☐ 出太阳了，今天是晴天。

➡ _____

② ☐ 外面下着雪，天气很热。

➡ _____

③ ☐ Ⓐ：明天天气好吗？ Ⓑ：我想明天会雨天。

➡ _____

④ ☐ 没事做，我就去图书馆看书。

➡ _____

⑤ ☐ 我们一起去球场打球怎么了？

➡ _____

6 Go to *Exercise* > *Sentence Quiz* in your [Go 300] to take the quiz. Choose the best two results.

TYPING RECORDS		Date	Accurate Spelling per Minute	Three Most Common Mistakes (Character)
	Record 1			
		Level	Time Elapsed	
		Date	Accurate Spelling per Minute	Three Most Common Mistakes (Character)
	Record 2			
		Level	Time Elapsed	

7 Practice the strokes to write the characters.

yáng	zhe	xiào	fēng	yǔ
阳	着	笑	风	雨

出太＿＿＿，花看＿＿＿阳光＿＿＿；

＿＿＿yáng＿＿＿＿＿＿＿zhe＿＿＿＿＿＿＿＿xiào

刮＿＿＿、下＿＿＿，草地上的花都在跳舞。

＿＿fēng＿＿＿＿＿＿yǔ

阳 阳 阳 阳 阳 阳

阳	阳	阳			

着 着 着 着 着 着 着 着 着 着

着	着	着			

笑 笑 笑 笑 笑 笑 笑 笑 笑 笑

笑	笑	笑			

风 风 风 风

风	风	风			

雨 雨 雨 雨 雨 雨 雨 雨

雨	雨	雨			

8a

According to the weather forecast in the area where you live, fill in the forecast for the following week in the table below.

Date 今天	＿＿月 ＿＿日 星期＿＿	＿＿月 ＿＿日 星期＿＿	＿＿月 ＿＿日 星期＿＿	＿＿月 ＿＿日 星期＿＿	＿＿月 ＿＿日 星期＿＿	＿＿月 ＿＿日 星期＿＿	＿＿月 ＿＿日 星期＿＿
Icons of Weather Forecast							
Temperature							
Weather Forecast*							

* Write the weather forecast in Chinese.

Sunny Day   Rainy Day   Cloudy Day   Windy Day   Snowy Day

8b

Answer the following questions in Chinese.

❶ 星期几会下雨?

_____

❷ 星期几是晴天?

_____

❸ 哪一天最冷?

_____

❹ 哪一天最热?

_____

❺ 星期六和星期日天气好不好? 你要去哪里?

_____

REVIEW 2

1 In the right column, circle the phrases which are in the same tone as the phrase in the left column.

①	晴天	新闻	阳光	开车	雨天
②	运动	外面	球赛	爱好	下课
③	刮风	一边	阴天	分钟	喜欢
④	电影	走路	跳舞	电视	对面
⑤	精彩	心情	新闻	音乐	孙女
⑥	紧张	打架	表哥	一边	打开
⑦	所以	左转	小考	自己	球场
⑧	吵架	生气	右转	比赛	美丽

2 Fill in the blanks with the words provided.

a
- **A** 紧张
- **B** 精彩
- **C** 电影
- **D** 唱歌
- **E** 下雨
- **F** 爱好
- **G** 晴天

1 姐姐喜欢跳舞，跳舞是她的_____。

2 今天下午是阴天，我想晚上会_____。

3 因为哥哥常常参加球赛，所以他不会_____。

4 我看什么_____，妹妹就看什么_____。

5 他跳的舞真_____，我也想学跳舞。

b
- **A** 很少
- **B** 有时
- **C** 常常

1 我很喜欢看不同的书，我_____去图书馆看书。

2 姐姐的球队打得很好，他们参加球赛_____输，常常拿冠军(champion)。

3 叔叔家和我家很近，_____我去叔叔家，_____叔叔来我家。

4 每天下午五点钟，弟弟要看卡通，哥哥要看电影，所以他们_____吵架。

3 Circle the correct answer.

① 下午我看了一场很（请彩 / 精彩）的球赛。

② 今天是（晴天 / 晴天），我们可以去打球。

③ 我每个星期去外婆家（两次 / 两冷）。

④ 我们都喜欢参加学校的课外（话动 / 活动）。

⑤ 电视（节日 / 节目）真好看，可是不要看太久。

4 Each sentence has a number of missing words which are identical. Identify the missing words and fill in the blanks.

① 你住在哪个城 ⬚ ？这个城 ⬚ 有没有 ⬚ 场？

② 这台电脑很 ⬚ 宜，有电脑真方 ⬚ 。

③ 张 ⬚ 嘴多说，打 ⬚ 书多看，打 ⬚ 电脑 ⬚ 心学。

④ 弟弟的爱 ⬚ 是跳舞，他的舞跳得很 ⬚ 。

⑤ 夏天到了，我 ⬚ 了种花，还要 ⬚ 草。

⑥ 看 ⬚ 视，打 ⬚ 话，用 ⬚ 脑，有电 (electricity) 真方便。

⑦ 我的中文说 ⬚ 不好，我 ⬚ 用心学。

5 Answer the questions in complete sentence in Chinese according to the descriptions provided.

1 我们都爱看卡通，弟弟一个星期看180分钟，表妹一个星期看两个小时，我每天看20分钟。

Who spends the longest time watching cartoons per week?

_____

2 哥哥要参加球赛，他不会紧张，可是妈妈说她很紧张。比赛那天，爸爸紧张得走来走去，妈妈对爸爸说："我看你比我还紧张。"

Who is most nervous about Older Brother taking part in the ball game?

_____

3 哥哥比表哥大两岁，堂哥比哥哥大五岁。

In the diagram, who is 哥哥, 表哥, and 堂哥? Label them.

4 A比B高，D比B矮，D比C高。

Label the people in the diagram A, B, C, and D according to the description above.

6 Translate the following questions into Chinese. Then answer the questions in Chinese according to the pictures.

A : What kinds of television programs do you like to watch?

1

Translation: _____

B : _____

A : How is the weather today?

2

Translation: _____

B : _____

A : Are you nervous about taking part in the ball game?

3 Translation: _____

B : _____ （不会）

A : _____

4 **B** : If it is rainy, I won't go to play basketball.

Translation: _____